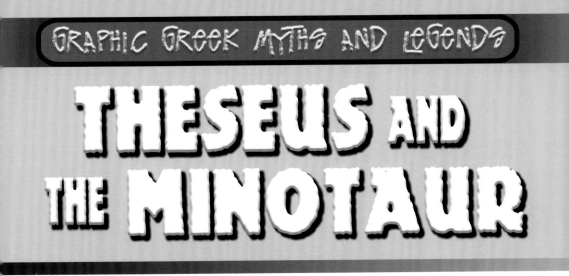

GRAPHIC GREEK MYTHS AND LEGENDS

THESEUS AND THE MINOTAUR

By Gilly Cameron Cooper

Consultant: Dr. Nick Saunders,
University College London

WORLD ALMANAC® LIBRARY

Please visit our web site at: www.garethstevens.com
For a free color catalog describing World Almanac® Library's list of high-quality books
and multimedia programs, call 1-800-848-2928 (USA) or 1-800-387-3178 (Canada).
World Almanac® Library's fax: (414) 332-3567.

Library of Congress Cataloging-in-Publication Data available upon request from publisher.
Fax (414) 336-0157 for the attention of the Publishing Records Department.

ISBN-13: 978-0-8368-7749-6 (lib. bdg.)
ISBN-13: 978-0-8368-8149-3 (softcover)

This North America edition first published in 2007 by
World Almanac® Library
A Member of the WRC Media Family of Companies
330 West Olive Street, Suite 100
Milwaukee, WI 53212 USA

Illustrators: Bookmatrix

World Almanac® Library managing editor: Valerie J. Weber
World Almanac® Library art direction: Tammy West

Printed in Canada

1 2 3 4 5 6 7 8 9 10 10 09 08 07 06

CONTENTS

THE GREEKS, THEIR GODS, & MYTHS

The world of the ancient Greeks was bound by the Mediterranean Sea and the rugged lands surrounding it. It was a place of dangerous winds and sudden storms. The ancient Greeks saw their lives as controlled by spirits of nature and the gods. They told myths about how the gods fought with each other and created the universe. These stories helped explain what caused natural events, such as lightning and earthquakes, and the fates of individuals.

The ancient Greeks believed that 12 gods and goddesses ruled over the world. The 10 gods and goddesses shown on the next page are the most important ones. Some of them appear in this myth.

The ancient Greek gods and goddesses looked and acted like human beings. They fell in love, were jealous and vain, and argued with each other. But unlike humans, they were immortal. They did not die but lived forever. They also had superhuman strength and specific magical powers. Each god or goddess controlled certain forces of nature or aspects of human life, such as marriage or hunting.

In the myths, the gods had their favorite humans. Sometimes, the gods even had children with these people. Their children were thus half gods. They were usually mortal, which meant that they could die. It also meant that they had some special powers, too. When their human children were in trouble, the gods would help them.

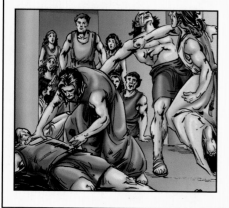

The gods liked to meddle in human life and took sides with different people. The gods also liked to play tricks on humans. They did so for many reasons—because it was fun; because they would gain something; or because they wanted to get even with someone.

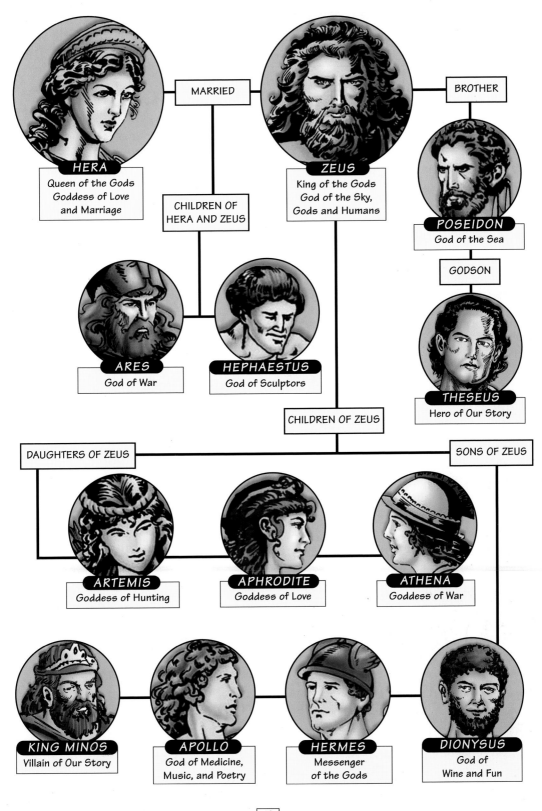

HERA
Queen of the Gods
Goddess of Love
and Marriage

MARRIED

ZEUS
King of the Gods
God of the Sky,
Gods and Humans

BROTHER

POSEIDON
God of the Sea

CHILDREN OF
HERA AND ZEUS

GODSON

ARES
God of War

HEPHAESTUS
God of Sculptors

THESEUS
Hero of Our Story

CHILDREN OF ZEUS

DAUGHTERS OF ZEUS

SONS OF ZEUS

ARTEMIS
Goddess of Hunting

APHRODITE
Goddess of Love

ATHENA
Goddess of War

KING MINOS
Villain of Our Story

APOLLO
God of Medicine,
Music, and Poetry

HERMES
Messenger
of the Gods

DIONYSUS
God of
Wine and Fun

HOW THE MYTH BEGINS

Our story opens with two powerful men, both with strong links to the gods. King Minos's father was Zeus, lord of the skies. Both of Theseus's parents were human, but he was also the godson of Poseidon, god of the sea.

At the time of our story, King Minos was the most powerful and wealthy ruler of ancient Greece. His palace was on the island of Crete. From here, King Minos controlled the most important trade routes in the Mediterranean Sea. In contrast, the other Greek kingdoms were small and poor. Their rulers changed often, making the kingdoms easy targets. Thus King Minos could bully the people of the other kingdoms and demand money—and other forms of wealth.

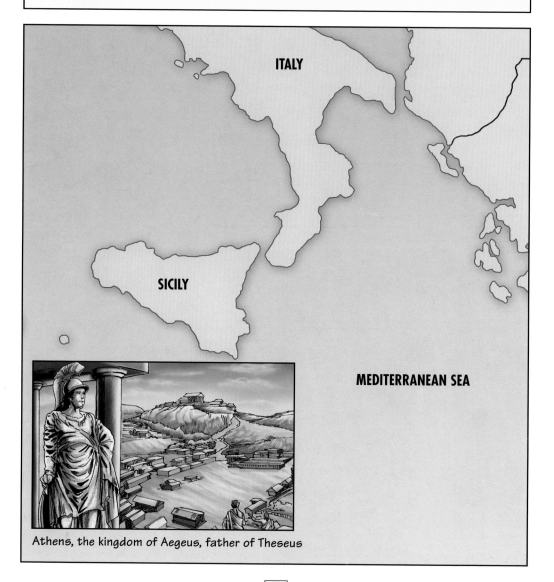

ITALY

SICILY

MEDITERRANEAN SEA

Athens, the kingdom of Aegeus, father of Theseus

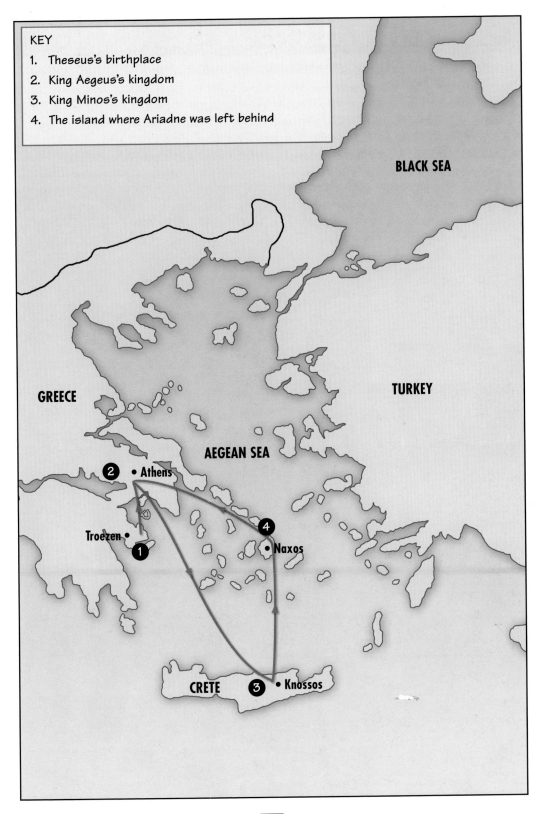

KEY
1. Theseus's birthplace
2. King Aegeus's kingdom
3. King Minos's kingdom
4. The island where Ariadne was left behind

BLACK SEA

GREECE

TURKEY

AEGEAN SEA

2 • Athens

Troezen •

1

4

• Naxos

CRETE **3** • Knossos

BIRTH OF A HERO

Theseus's parents were Aegeus, king of Athens, and Princess Aethra of Troezen. As son of the king, Theseus would inherit the throne of Athens. But Aegeus and Aethra could not be together for long. Different groups of people were fighting for control of Athens. Aegeus had to return to his kingdom. The night Aegeus left, Aethra went to Poseidon's temple. Poseidon was lord of the sea and guardian god of Troezen. Poseidon agreed to become godfather to Aethra's unborn child.

Bring our child up here in secret. It would be too dangerous for him in Athens. My brother's sons would kill a son of mine to stop him from having my throne.

Their child will be great and worthy of my protection.

Aegeus asked Aethra to hide his sandals and a dagger under a large rock. He went back to Athens. Nine months later, Theseus was born.

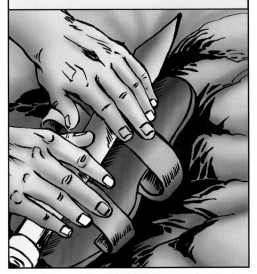

Princess Aethra would not say who Theseus's father was. People thought he must be Poseidon's son. When Theseus was older, Aethra decided he was ready for the truth.

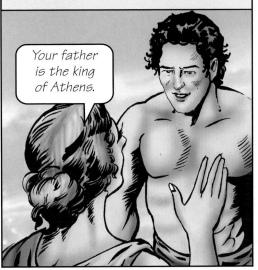

Your father is the king of Athens.

Aethra told Theseus about the rock where his father's sandals and dagger were hidden.

I must go to my father in Athens and claim my place as his son and heir. These things will show him I am his true son.

Theseus could have sailed to Athens, but he wanted to prove he was brave. So he took the long road to Athens. Dangerous villains lurked along the winding road.

Very soon, Theseus met a bandit. This evil man crushed anyone who crossed his path with a huge spiked club. Theseus tackled and defeated him. He then seized the weapon and battered the man to death with it. Theseus kept the club. It would prove to be very useful. . . .

The next problem for Theseus was a man known as "Pine-bender." He would pull together a couple of trees, then tie people between them. The trees would spring back and tear the victims apart. Our hero overpowered Pine-bender and got rid of him forever.

Theseus then came to a narrow path at the top of a high cliff. Far below, waves crashed against the rocks. A mean-looking man blocked his way. The man forced people to wash his feet. As soon as they bent down to do it, he kicked them over the cliff. In the sea below, a giant, flesh-eating turtle was waiting to eat them. Theseus picked the man up and threw him over the cliff.

WELCOME TO ATHENS

News of Theseus's adventures and strength reached Athens. A feast was held for him at the palace. Now an old man, King Aegeus had married another woman named Medea. Together they had a son. Medea instantly knew who Theseus was. She also knew that he might prevent her son from becoming king. She told Aegeus that Theseus was dangerous and he should poison his wine.

That man is a dangerous spy and killer. You must poison his wine.

No! That's my knife, the one I left in Troezen. He is my son. By Zeus, don't touch his wine.

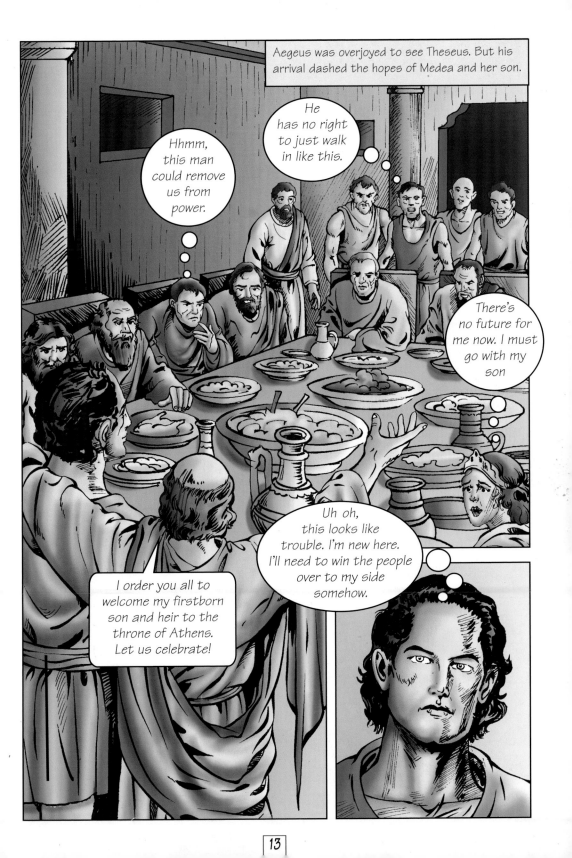

A chance soon arose for Theseus to impress the Athenians. For many years, a fire-breathing bull had brought terror to them. It had killed hundreds of people. One of its first victims had been the son of the most powerful king in the lands surrounding the Aegean Sea, Minos of Crete. . . .

THE CHOSEN FEW

Soon after Theseus's arrival in Athens, it was time for the third payment. King Minos sailed from Crete to make sure that the Athenians offered its best young people. They nervously gathered with their parents in the city square. They drew lots to decide who would go to Crete. Their parents were furious that King Aegeus's son Theseus was not taking part.

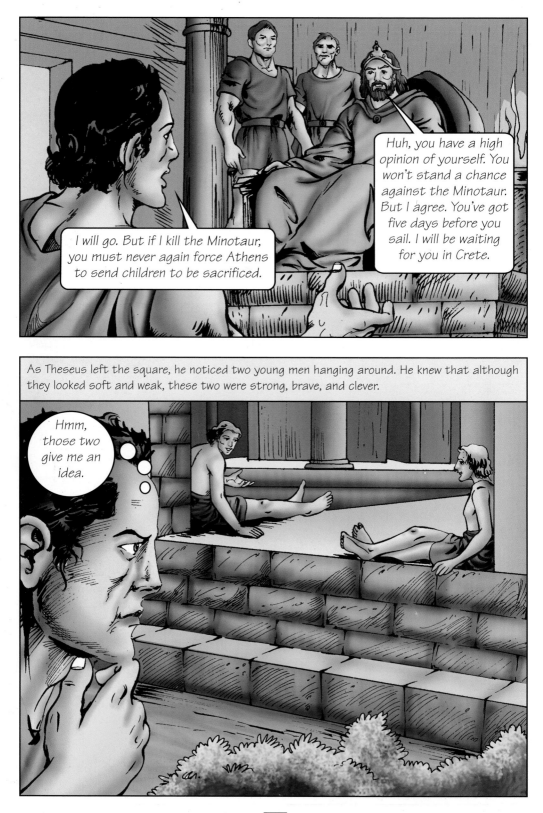

As Theseus left the square, he noticed two young men hanging around. He knew that although they looked soft and weak, these two were strong, brave, and clever.

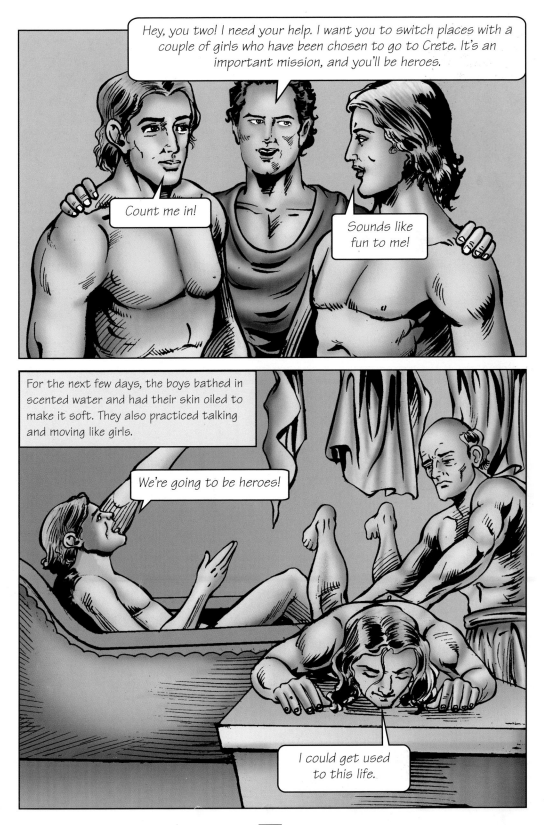

On the sixth of April, the chosen boys and girls gathered in the square. Disguised as girls, the two brave boys joined the victims. Theseus grabbed a couple of the real chosen girls.

Quick, run home and hide. These two will take your places. Don't tell anyone!

Thank you so much!

Theseus led the 14 young people and their mothers to a temple to pray.

Please protect us.

The Minotaur sounds awful. We're all going to die.

The sad group dragged their feet as they walked to the waiting ship.

The mothers brought baskets of food and fruit for the journey. They told their frightened children stories of heroes and heroines to give them courage.

Be brave, children. The monster might not be as awful as you think.

Because of the sad purpose of the journey, the crew put up black sails.

HEAVE

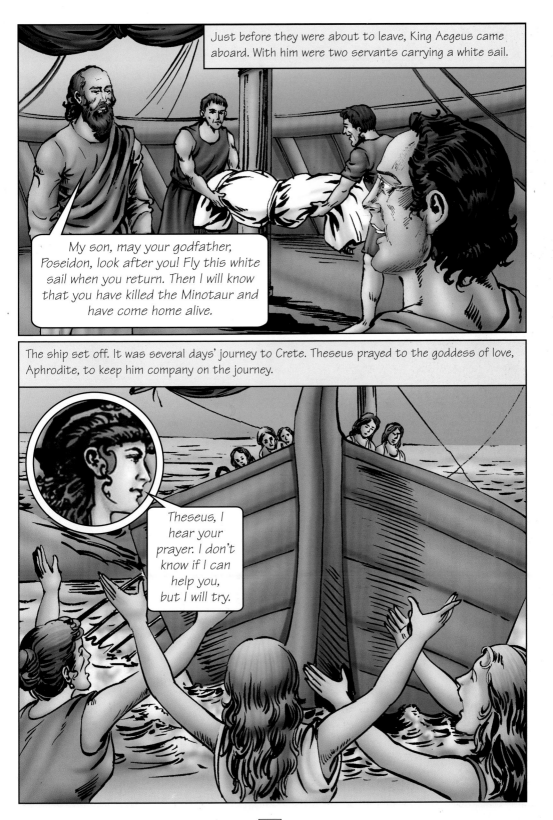

Just before they were about to leave, King Aegeus came aboard. With him were two servants carrying a white sail.

My son, may your godfather, Poseidon, look after you! Fly this white sail when you return. Then I will know that you have killed the Minotaur and have come home alive.

The ship set off. It was several days' journey to Crete. Theseus prayed to the goddess of love, Aphrodite, to keep him company on the journey.

Theseus, I hear your prayer. I don't know if I can help you, but I will try.

THE FIRST CHALLENGE

Theseus and his companions were amazed by Knossos, the capital of Crete. The buildings and the clothes that people wore were so much more stylish than those in Athens. A big palace overlooked the town. They could see King Minos being carried down to them. He wanted to make sure that all 14 victims had arrived. Filled with fear, the boys and girls prepared to land.

Minos counted and checked the Athenians. He didn't notice the two boys disguised as girls. Perhaps this was because his eyes had stopped on one, very pretty girl.

The king ordered to be set down at once. He was stiff after sitting in the chair and staggered to his feet. He wanted this girl for himself, even though he already had a wife.

Ha ha ha! Poseidon wouldn't care. Besides, I don't believe you're his godson.

Minos took a heavy gold ring from his finger and threw it into the deep, dark blue waters of the harbor.

Prove you are Poseidon's godson by bringing back this gold ring. See if your so-called godfather helps you find it!

Theseus didn't know how to call his godfather for help. He needed time to think.

First, Minos, prove that you are a godson of Zeus.

Minos immediately called Zeus. There was a flash of lightning and a loud clap of thunder from Zeus, lord of the sky.

Father Zeus, hear me!

Once the sky was clear again, Theseus plunged into the water. Dolphins immediately came to help Theseus, guiding him to the ring. On the dock, Princess Ariadne was watching. She was the lovely daughter of King Minos. Aphrodite began forming a plan to help Theseus.

Poseidon sent his queen, Amphitrite, and her sea nymphs. They began to search for the ring. They found it lying between rocks. Amphitrite also gave Theseus a beautiful crown of delicate golden leaves and jewels. It had been her wedding present from the goddess of love, Aphrodite. It was extra proof that Poseidon was Theseus's godfather.

Theseus burst out of the water, holding up the ring and the crown.

LOVERS UNITE

King Minos ordered his guards to take Theseus and the 13 others to his palace. A massive sculpture of bull horns above the main entrance reminded them of what was to come. Smooth black stone covered the floors of the courtyard and rooms. The walls and columns were painted in rich colors. The prisoners were locked in a room. Ariadne bribed a guard so she could talk to Theseus.

Ariadne explained that the Minotaur lived in the center of a labyrinth. It was a maze of false turns and secret passages. People got lost in it and died. She offered some magic thread to Thesus. She told him to tie it to the entrance of the labyrinth. The thread would never run out and would lead Theseus back out of the labyrinth. Asterius the Minotaur lived in the center of the maze. To get to him, Theseus must only make left turns.

I'll help you get out of here alive if you marry me and take me back to Athens.

Of course I'll marry you. I think you're wonderful.

Theseus doesn't have a chance against the Minotaur. We're all going to die.

Theseus decided to go into the labyrinth immediately. He was allowed to take his club. No one expected him to get out alive anyway. Theseus pushed open the labyrinth door and stepped into the darkness.

All around Theseus were high walls that twisted and turned, confusing paths, and dead ends. Every direction looked the same. He felt the walls were closing in on him. Whenever he had a choice of directions, he turned left, never right, as Ariadne had suggested. Sometimes he stumbled over the bones of other people who had not found their way out. He kept checking that the magic thread was unwinding behind him.

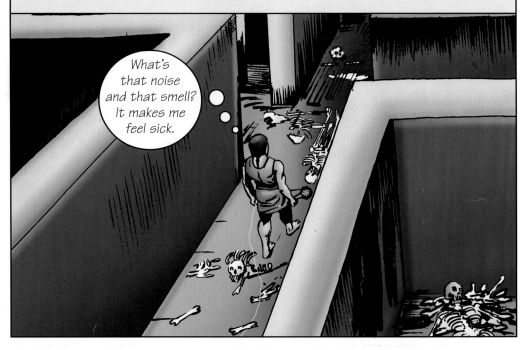

What a disgusting creature.

Finally Theseus stumble into a courtyard. At one side was Asterius, asleep. He was a huge man with a massive bull's head. Theseus knew that those deadly horns had ripped out the insides of many Athenian girls and boys.

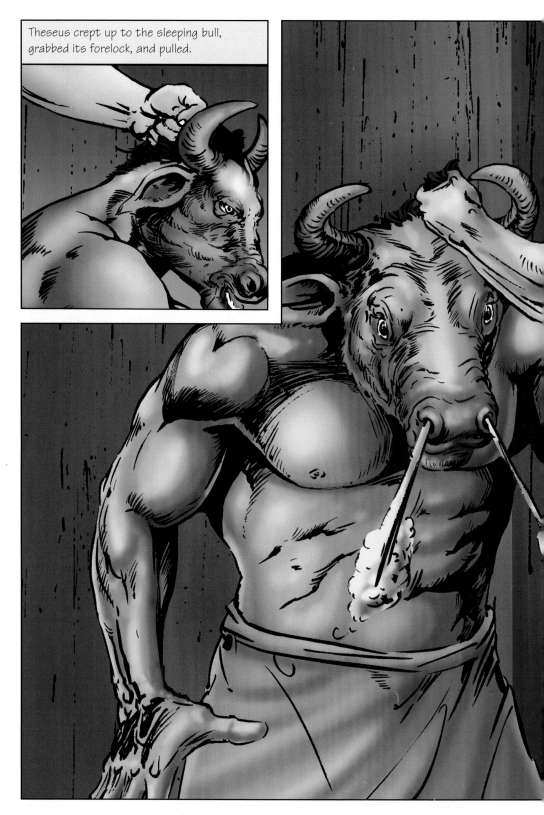

Theseus crept up to the sleeping bull, grabbed its forelock, and pulled.

With a wild roar, the Minotaur awoke and leaped to his feet. Theseus clung to the monster's forelock. The Minotaur whipped him back and forth in midair.

Suddenly, Theseus let go and flew through the air, doing a neat backflip. He landed on his feet.

The Minotaur was so surprised that it only took Theseus one blow with his famous club to kill the monster.

To please his godfather, Theseus immediately offered the bull as a sacrifice to Poseidon. He cut off the bull's head. Carrying the head, he then followed the thread all the way out of the labyrinth.

I offer the blood of the Minotaur to my godfather, Poseidon.

A SNEAKY ESCAPE

While Theseus was in the labyrinth, the two boys disguised as girls had freed themselves and the other Athenians. Then they leaped upon the guards, surprising them completely. The boys took the guards' weapons and killed the men.

They rowed the ship to keep from waking anyone in the city. Thirty oars cut silently through the smooth black waters until they were safely away.

Set sail for Athens!

After several days of sailing, a storm forced the ship onto the island of Naxos. It was late. They decided to rest on the island until the storm passed.

The storm is too strong.

They awoke the next morning to good weather. Theseus was eager to set sail again and went to check the ship. The others were awake, too, and followed him. But Ariadne was so comfortable on the soft grass that she kept sleeping.

That beautiful woman should be my wife. I'd be a better husband than Theseus. After all, I am a god.

The god of wine, Dionysus, cast a spell on Theseus to make him forget that Ariadne ever existed.

After a time, the sleeping Ariadne stirred. She rubbed her eyes and yawned. Then her stomach sunk—she was completely alone. Faraway, out to sea, a ship with black sails was moving swiftly away. Theseus had left her! Not only had he dumped her, he had left her alone on a strange and unknown island!

Meanwhile, the ship carrying Theseus and the others was close to Athens. Everyone was looking forward to being home.

Theseus, you will be given a hero's parade.

Hooray!

Look, I can see the cliffs! We're home at last.

On shore stood King Aegeus. He had been looking out to sea every day. He was waiting for the white sail that would signal the safe return of Theseus.

No! It can't be true! The ship's sail is black. My son is dead.

But Theseus had forgotten to fly the white sail. A black sail rose above the horizon.

Thinking that his son was dead, Aegeus threw himself over the cliff to his death in the sea below. In this way, the gods punished Theseus for leaving Ariadne behind. Theseus had just found his father. Now, that father was gone.

The ship landed. Theseus led the way with the two disguised boys. The celebrations began. No one could bear to tell Theseus that his father had died.

As soon as the parade was over, Theseus was told of his father's tragic death. He was very sad and built a shrine to the old king.

Theseus agreed to rule in his father's place. He became King of Athens and was a wise ruler. He brought together the different, fighting groups in Athens and kept away enemies.

As for Ariadne, she married the god Dionysus. They had many children and lived happily on the beautiful island of Naxos. Dionysus was so happy that he blessed the island. Even today it is the greenest island in the Cyclades.

GLOSSARY

bandit *a violent criminal who steals from other people*

city-state *a city or village and the surrounding area with its own leader, laws, and government*

Cyclades *a group of islands in the southern Aegean Sea, of which Naxos is the largest*

feast *a party for a particular reason, usually involving lots of food and drink*

forelock *a strand of hair that grows just above the forehead*

godfather *a person who is chosen to look after a child that is not his own*

guardian god *a god that is chosen or believed to have a special responsibility for protecting a place or a person*

heir *the person who has been chosen to receive the property, money, or title (such as* king*) of a person who has died. Children are often the heirs to their parents' property.*

immortal *living forever, like the gods*

inherit *to receive property, money, or title (such as* king*) when someone dies*

labyrinth *a maze or confusing network of passages or paths in which it is difficult to find one's way*

lots *marked objects chosen from a pile by individuals to decide a question*

lottery *a drawing of lots used to decide an issue*

Minoan *A civilization named after its most famous king, Minos, and centered on the island of Crete in the southern Aegean Sea. Minoan power was based on successful trade and great wealth.*

mission *an important job that is sometimes secret*

mortal *having a life that is ended by death, usually referring to humans as distinct from immortal gods.*

myths *the stories of a tribe or people that tell of their gods, goddesses, heroes, and turning points in their history*

nymphs *minor divine beings of nature that usually live in the water, forests, or mountains*

revenge *to get even for something done wrong to a person*

sacrifice *to offer something, such as a specially killed animal, to a god in the hope of winning the god's support*

shrine *a memorial that people visit*

temple *a building where gods are worshipped*

BOOKS

Byrd, Robert. *The Hero and the Minotaur*. New York: Dutton Children's Books, 2005.

Ford, James Evelyn. *Theseus and the Minotaur*. Ancient Myths (series). Minneapolis: Picture Window Books, 2004.

McCaughrean, Geraldine. *Theseus*. Heroes (series) Chicago: Cricket Books, 2005.

Spinner, Stephanie. *Monster in the Maze: The Story of the Minotaur*. All Aboard Reading (series). New York: Grosset & Dunlap, 2000.

Welvaert, Scott R. *Theseus and the Minotaur*. World Mythology (series). Mankato, MN: Capstone Press, 2006.

WEB SITES

Encyclopedia of Greek Mythology
www.mythweb.com/encyc/entries/ theseus.html
Learn more about Theseus's story.

Mythical Weird Beasts — The Minotaur
web.ukonline.co.uk/conker/weird-beasts/ minotaur.htm
The story of Theseus in the maze of the Minotaur

Publishers note to educators and parents: Our editors have carefully reviewed these Web sites to ensure that they are suitable for children. Many Web sites change frequently, however, and we cannot guarantee that a site's future contents will continue to meet our high standards of quality and educational value. Be advised that children should be closely supervised whenever they access the Internet.

INDEX